What Would YOU Do?

Should Charlotte Share?

Being a Good Friend

Rebecca Rissman

Raintree is an imprint of Capstone Global Library Limited, a company incorporated in England and Wales having its registered office at 7 Pilgrim Street, London, EC4V 6LB – Registered company number: 6695582

To contact Raintree:
Phone: 0845 6044371
Fax: + 44 (0) 1865 312263
Email: myorders@raintreepublishers.co.uk
Outside the UK please telephone +44 1865 312262.

First published in hardback in 2013

Edited by Daniel Nunn, Rebecca Rissman, and Siân Smith
Designed by Steve Mead
Picture research by Mica Brancic
Production by Alison Parsons
Originated by Capstone Global Library Ltd
Printed and bound in China by Leo Paper Products Ltd

ISBN 978 1 406 25329 0
16 15 14 13 12
10 9 8 7 6 5 4 3 2 1

British Library Cataloguing in Publication Data
Rissman, Rebecca.
Should Charlotte share?. -- (What would you do?)
1. Sharing--Juvenile literature.
I. Title II. Series
302.1'4-dc23

Acknowledgements
All photographs © Capstone Publishers (Karon Dubke).

Every effort has been made to contact copyright holders of material reproduced in this book. Any omissions will be rectified in subsequent printings if notice is given to the publisher.

Contents

Making choices

We make choices every day, such as "When should I do my homework?"

Our choices have effects.

Ask yourself if your choices will have good or bad effects.

Should Charlotte share?

Charlotte has lots of extra orange slices. Should Charlotte share?

Charlotte could choose to share her orange slices.

Charlotte could choose not to share her orange slices.

What would YOU have done?

If Charlotte had shared her orange slices, she and her friends could have enjoyed the snack together. If Charlotte had eaten them all herself, it could have made her friends feel sad and they might choose not to share with Charlotte in the future.

Should Henry help?

Henry's sister's shoes are untied.
Should Henry help?

Henry could choose to help his sister tie her shoes.

Henry could choose not to help
his sister to tie her shoes.

What would YOU have done?

If Henry had helped his sister to tie her shoes, he could have made her happy and they could have played together. If Henry had not helped her, she might have fallen and hurt herself.

Should Wendy tease her teammate?

Wendy has a new person on her sports team. Should Wendy tease her teammate?

Wendy could choose to tease her new teammate.

Wendy could choose to be kind to her new teammate.

What would YOU have done?

If Wendy had teased her new teammate, she would have hurt her feelings. Other people would have thought that Wendy was not very nice. If Wendy had chosen to be kind to her new teammate, she might have made a new friend!

Should Theo tell the truth?

Theo broke his friend's toy. Should Theo tell the truth?

Theo could choose to lie.

Theo could choose to tell the truth.

What would YOU have done?

If Theo had lied, he might have got his friend into trouble. His friend and others might not believe him in the future – even when he tells the truth. If Theo had told the truth and said he was sorry his friend could have forgiven him.

Picture glossary

choice a decision

effects the results of a decision or something you choose to do. Choices can have good or bad effects.

lie to say something that is not true

truth something that is real or correct

Index

Notes for parents and teachers

Before reading

Explain to children that a consequence is the outcome, or result, of a decision. Explain that different decisions can have different consequences, and that some are better than others. Write a question on the board, for example, *What should Alsena eat for lunch?* Ask the children to suggest several different options and record these on the board, for example, *salad, sweets, nothing,* and *pizza*. Ask children to think of possible outcomes for each choice. For example under *Sweets* you might write, *Could get a stomach ache*.

After reading

Show children how to make a chart with two columns. Label the left column *Decision* and the right column *Outcome*. Encourage children to fill their chart out once a day to track their decisions and the results.